THE HERITAGE COLLECTION

THE BOOK KING

The Story of Tom Warth and Books for Africa

Rosemond Sarpong Owens

Lion's Historian
PRESS
Amplifying Authentic Voices

The Book King : The Story of Tom Warth
and Books For Africa

Copyright © 2023 by Rosemond Sarpong Owens

Layout designer: Nassim Sarkar

Illustrator: Amina Yaqoob

Library of Congress Control Number: 978-1-956051-21-6

ISBN 978-1-956051-24-7 (hardcover)
ISBN 978-1-956051-21-6 (paperback)
ISBN 978-1-956051-22-3 (ebook)

Published by Lion's Historian Press
https://www.lionshistorian.net/

This book is dedicated to

Mabel and Tom

Contents

Chapter 1

Tom's Curious Childhood

O nce upon a time, in a quaint town near Cambridge, England, lived a boy named Tom. His parents, Ewart and Olive Mary Warth, filled his childhood with wonder and adventure. Tom spent his days playing with his younger brother, John, and their loyal pet dog. But what Tom cherished most were the books that whisked him away to distant lands in thrilling escapades. Little did he know that his boundless love for books would one day touch the lives of children around the globe.

Chapter 2

The Boarding School Adventure

As Tom grew, he faced fresh challenges when he was sent to a boarding school. He tried his hand at French and Latin, experimented with the clarinet. Tom's heart was always aflame with a spirit of adventure. He even even traded his clarinet for an audacious adventure in France.

4

Chapter 3

Off to America!

In 1959, Tom received an extraordinary opportunity. A friend offered to help him visit America. With excitement, Tom packed his bags and stepped onto American soil in 1960. Tom went from New York to Minnesota , Arizona to North Carolina. This experience would reshape his life forever. Tom decided to live in America.

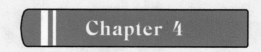

Chapter 4

The Car Enthusiast

Tom grew a passion for cars, just like his father. He embarked on thrilling escapades, hitchhiking to the Mardi Gras in New Orleans. Tom acquired a Volkswagen Beetle in Winnipeg, which he used to discover small towns in the area. Tom's love for cars eventually transformed into a successful business, yet his dreams knew no bounds.

A Letter from Africa

One fateful day, Tom received a mysterious letter. It came from someone in Africa who suggested a family connection to Tom. This letter sparked Tom's curiosity about Africa, setting him on a completely new adventure. Africa was about to weave itself into the very fabric of his life, but Tom had no idea of the incredible journey ahead.

Chapter 6

Journey to Uganda

Tom's African travels began when he met Loy Zabasajja, a woman from Uganda who was visiting his children in Minnesota. Tom promised her that he would come to Africa to see her one day. Tom kept his promise and traveled to Uganda to see Loy. They explored her hometown of Jinja, Uganda. Their path led them to a local library with nearly bare shelves and worn-out, tattered books. Tom was deeply moved and resolved to act. This encounter marked the start of his remarkable voyage to bring books to Africa to provide children with more access to reading materials.

The Birth of Books For Africa

Inspired by the library in Uganda, Tom felt compelled to make a difference. He invited all his buddies to the table and they initiated the practice of sending boxes filled with books to Africa, and the impact was nothing short of magical. This marked the birth of *Books For Africa*, an organization dedicated to delivering books to schools and libraries across the African continent.

Chapter 8

Challenges and Triumphs

Running Books For Africa had its share of obstacles, but with a devoted team, steadfast supporters, and countless volunteers, the organization met these challenges head-on with determination. The books sent were just what the receiving group needed. Books for Africa celebrated each success with more deliveries across Africa. With every shipment, Books for Africa realized it was making a difference in many lives.

Chapter 9

Tom's Extraordinary Walks

Tom took incredible walks to raise funds for Books For Africa, having walked for 2,000 miles. Tom walked across the Gambia (West Africa). He climbed Mt. Kilimanjaro in Tanzania for his 70th birthday. When he turned 80 years old, he returned to Tanzania and visited Zanzibar Island, walking from one end of the island to the other.

Closer to home, Tom has walked in Minnesota, Wisconsin, and from the Canadian border to Iowa. He's even hiked up Eagle Mountain on the North Shore of Lake Superior. But guess what? Tom's not alone on these walks. Several of his friends and Books For Africa supporters joined him on these walks.

Chapter 10

Books, Ebooks, and Law Books for Africa

Books For Africa didn't just stick to sending physical books; they also embraced the digital age, sending electronic books, known as Ebooks, to reach even more people. Furthermore, they introduced a special program called the *Law and Democracy Initiative*, sharing law books to help strengthen the rule of law in Africa. Their dedication to spreading knowledge continues, ensuring that schools and libraries have access to a wide variety of books.

20

Chapter 11

Tom Warth's Enduring Legacy

Tom's Books For Africa journey has been marked by impressive walks, mountain-climbing adventures, and a deep commitment to the organization he started. He remains a steadfast believer in the transformative power of real books, inspiring others to join him in various walks and mountain climbs around the world. Tom's legacy endures as he continues to inspire people to support Books For Africa in countless ways. He firmly believes that every child in Africa should have access to a book, igniting a shared commitment to contribute to literacy on the African continent. His ongoing mission serves as a testament to the fact that one person's passion and determination can transform countless lives.

Chapter 12

Celebrating 35 Years of Books For Africa

In 2023, Books For Africa threw the biggest party ever! They had joyful celebrations, exciting gatherings, and collected heaps of books . People from all around the world joined in to celebrate Books For Africa's incredible journey, which has already sent a whopping 59 million books to every corner of Africa. But the party wasn't just about looking back; Tom had a challenge for everyone. He wanted them to do even more to help end the book famine in Africa.

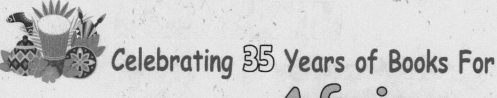

Celebrating 35 Years of Books For
Africa

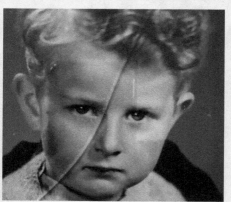

Books For Africa is the world's largest shipper of books to Africa, shipping over 50 million hard-copy and over 3 million digital books to Africa since 1988. Books For Africa's mission is to end the book famine in Africa.

Every one of the 55 countries on the African continent has received books shipped by Books For Africa. Donated books are collected from schools, libraries, universities, and private libraries and sorted in Books For Africa warehouses. Many languages are spoken across Africa, but English is one of the important common languages used to unite different regions and countries, and is widely taught in schools across the continent. While most books sent are in English, books in other languages such as French, Portuguese, Spanish, Swahili, and Somali have also been sent as requested by partners in Africa.

For more information about Books For Africa, including how to donate books or funds, please visit www.booksforafrica.org.

Rosemond Sarpong Owens is founder of Lion's Historian Press, where we believe that every voice deserves to be heard. We are a publishing house dedicated to highlighting absent voices that have been missing from literature for centuries. Our mission is to create a more inclusive and diverse literary landscape, where everyone can see themselves represented in the stories they read.

At Lion's Historian Press, we understand the power of storytelling. We believe that books have the ability to shape our perceptions of the world, to inspire and educate, and to create empathy and understanding. That's why we are committed to publishing books that celebrate the rich diversity of our world and its people.

We are passionate about promoting diversity, equity, and inclusion in all aspects of our work. From our choice of authors and illustrators to the themes and topics we cover, we strive to represent the voices and perspectives that have been historically marginalized or excluded from mainstream literature. We are committed to creating a more equitable and just world, one book at a time.

Our founder, is inspired by the African proverb, "Until the lions have their own historians, the tale of the hunt will always glorify the hunter." She is on a mission to change the narrative, to give voice to those who have been silenced, and to empower readers of all ages and backgrounds to embrace their unique identities and experiences.

Our books range from children's stories to adult historical fiction Each book is carefully curated to offer a unique and diverse perspective on the world around us. Our books are not just for those who have been historically underrepresented in literature, but for anyone who believes in the power of storytelling to change the world.

We are committed to creating a world where every voice is heard and every story is told. We invite you to join us on this journey, to discover new voices and perspectives, and to help us create a more inclusive and equitable literary landscape.

References

- Books For Africa - Founder's Story

- Tom Warth: 50 Million Books and Counting on the Future of Africa

- Warth Celebrates 50 Years in America

- Author Conversations with Tom Warth (2019-2023) - Personal Interviews and Conversations with Tom Warth, Providing Valuable Insights and Stories for the Children's Book, "The Book King: The Story of Tom Warth and Books For Africa."

Acknowledgements

- Cover Photo Credit: *Dustin J. Holland, Better World Books.*

- Photo Gallery Credits: *Special thanks to Tom Warth for providing the images.*

- *Special thanks to Isaac Owens and Dr. Letitia De Graft Okyere for their editing contributions.*

- *Gratitude to Tom Warth for generously sharing his remarkable life story for this book*

Other Books in the Heritage Collection

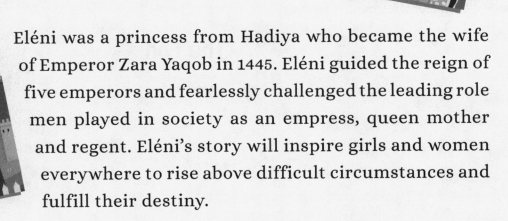

The story of Queen Amina is an important one for girls everywhere. Explore how Queen Amina gained a reputation as a fearless warrior, breaking barriers at a time when men dominated most aspects of life. Queen Amina's life will inspire and encourage you to be fearless.

Who was Queen Nandi? She is referred to as one of the greatest mothers that ever lived. As a queen mother, she saw her son Shaka become one of the greatest kings of the Zulu people and builder of the Zulu empire. Read her story and learn how she made her mark in history.

Eléni was a princess from Hadiya who became the wife of Emperor Zara Yaqob in 1445. Eléni guided the reign of five emperors and fearlessly challenged the leading role men played in society as an empress, queen mother and regent. Eléni's story will inspire girls and women everywhere to rise above difficult circumstances and fulfill their destiny.

R.J. Ghartey saw no limits to what he could achieve. As a young man, he rejected traditional paths of fishing and farming and learned a different trade. Through this, he became an influential business entrepreneur. In addition, Ghartey played an important role in local politics and found ways to improve the lives of those in his community. In telling Ghartey's story, the author hopes to encourage children with different dreams to pursue their destinies past challenges that they may face.

The End

Printed in the USA
CPSIA information can be obtained
at www.ICGtesting.com
LVHW080319251123
764833LV00007B/76